Poetry Series
Minnoor srinivasan
- poems -
Publication Date:
2021

A School Boy's Wonder

Temple elephant
All made in ivory
It makes me wonder.
Gandhi in the calendar
On wall
Laughs with a question.
My Mom's
Proud possession –
The ivory casket
Sheltering the costly
Jewels
Makes me wonder!
My grand pa's
Walking stick
With a grand grip
Carved in ivory
Bewitches the beholders,
As my grandpa
Glibly walks!
It makes me wonder!

My uncle presented
Me a tiny toy elephant
Resembling the stately
Man uses Nature
For his needy or greedy ends?

Becoming Arjuna

I implored the Mistress of poetic Vision, thus;
Grant me valor invincible
Like Arjuna of Mahabharata.
Seeing my anguish and quest
Pleading and plight, the Mistress obliged;
Talk to my mind's ear.
"You are devoured by desire.
Let me guide: grow in valor.
Take the subtle Bow of Life.
Having two ends with one string of
Equanimity
As two ends good and otherwise
Aspire to rise above petty whimper.
Have the target of Foe internal - Maya.
Illusion, the deceptive
Elusive Fish which is in whirl constant.
Let the arrow sharp,
The Meditation arrow Surge into
The realm - beyond,
Into the space Inner-
From being to Becoming
Yes. Becoming Arjuna! .

Call Back The Doves

Call back the doves,
yes.
The desire-doves,
Born of your mind,
Dove's flitting and flirting are
No more rewarding!
Tired of roaming vain
Call them back!
There is the vast blue
inscape.
Desire-dove, when
Chirping and singing
End in silence.
Let it rest
In the inner nest steeped
in silence
That excels the song,
In the nest of soul
Beyond minds
Bickering feeble!

Come On! Sing Merrily

When the hard rock clashes and
Danishes vehemently
Without any worry the creek sings
Sweet melodies mellifluously;
Even if difficulties dash against you
Come on sing like a creek!
Sing charmingly!
Black clouds in the sky
Bombard each other
Without any fear for the

Terrific thunderstorms
The lightning laughs at it
With a flash of a smile bright!
If troubles dash in your life
Happily laugh at them!
Bloom! Be cheerful!
Neither hurricane nor tempest
Can shake the Assembly of stars;
Without any fear, they smile brightly,
Driving away the darkness,
they adore the sky;
Whatever storm that meets you in life
Should never bother you!
Laugh away your worries!
Brighten up your mind!
Cheer up your heart!
Even if our hands bang and beat
The drum is never hurt;
It produces rhythmic treat
To make us dance with joy!
If misery and grief strike you
Please don't get shattered!
Let sweet music fill up your heart
Brush up suddenly!
Let your mind be absorbed in music
Come on! Sing merrily!

Darling Flower

Flower, Darling Flower!
Who made thee

In bower
Many colours and hues
Strangely who doth infuse!
Lord is He for one and all
Who made things big and small.

Doth Time Stay?
Time flows glibly
Into unseen strange world
Man feels constantly
'I am simply growing old'!
The clock shows time
Click- click it sings
Like turning book of pages
New experiences it brings!
Time abstract doth act
As it elopes with FAME
Yes, ponder! It is a fact
Day and night all a game!
Throb of heart doth warn
That TIME is up always
As man acts joyfully
Through ART and LOVE,
TIME stays.

Dream And Scheme
Meet and mingle
Never be single
Me and mine seeds
of Ego!

Erase the base.
Come out, with a
Mind stout!
From pulse to impulse
Let the note be fresh,
Out of your own mesh.
Go on web worldwide,
Make a stride,
Of soul's pride.
One and same
Creation's game.
From atom to cosmos,
Same Designer
Dream and scheme.
By one and same
One by Glorious one.
Mastered by
One Soul Supreme
Dream and scheme!

Drop The Drop

In the holy presence of
Lord Buddha,
His disciples gathered
In a mood awe-filled
The Lord presented a
Question poignant,
"If you are given
A drop of water
How would you preserve? "
With surprise all

Exclaimed,
"It is but a drop!
How can it be enduring? "
The Lord quibbled:
"Drop the drop
In the ocean bear, to bear!

Dust Bin

Dust bin dust bin
Put the rubbish in
Throw not elsewhere!
Put them in bin's care
All things, worn out
Wait for lorry stout
From time to time engage
Staff to clear garbage
Broken glass pieces of wood
Thrown away stale food
Stuffed it looks a glutton
puzzy cat even there leaps on
Bits of paper dirt and moss
Fills to brim as it was
Bin's belly then emptied
By staff prompt was indeed.

Eloquent In Dreams

Love! Is it ogling glance
Or a strange trance!
Love - mere word,
To conjure up a word
of the dream world!

Word,
Mirroring emotions
Half - human and half divine,
Love chirped by every
Bird,
Man - the love - bird
Has the song in bosom
As silence
Love is eloquent in
Dreams, than in
Reality.
Then guess - what is
The substance called
Love, the throb of
Being, beats to
Say: it is the weakness
Of the strong and
The strength of the weak!

Exist Find Exit

On the seashore
Crabs galore
Crawl and crawl
One and all.
Build their homes
Sandy and cozy.
Then and there
Build, exist
Momentarily.
The waves ruthless
Chase and dash
Sweeping the homes, smash!

Tenanting the house-hole
Comes and goes the tiny soul.
Willingly loses to,
The waves are scathing.
The crabs move bathing
Lose them unto
The fortunes on the shore
Drench and crawl
Bother! Not at all!

Fancy Cake

Cake, fancy cake
In many shapes they make
Ships and planes
Birds and cranes
Cake, fancy cake!
Santa's sledge
River and bridge
Cake, fancy cake
Much fun and fair
Stand we stare!
Love-birds are still
Keeping calm their bill
Buses double decker
All in plum and sugar!

Filling The Soul

Azure hills and deep dales
Wake to the note of nightingales!
The very air is just thrilled
Into peace, my soul is filled.

And then I greet the ridge
Wrapped in fog and bridge
That connects people to meet
All souls seem to gladly greet!
Bud and big-lipped flower
Greet the visitors in bower
A bird lonely sits on a tower
Dreaming perhaps of happy hour!
Love flows in the dry soul
Makes it alive to pouring joyful
Where do every being find refuge?
Nature is bountiful ,
fabulous and huge!

Fish Tub

Fish, at their own sweet whim
Softly glide, move and swim,
Colors feasting frenzied eye,
Make also fine attire simply
Creating bubbles the fish play well
Leaving onlookers in Beauty's spell!
Exotic hues dots and lines
Of fish dash in aqua shines!
Thus full of patterns charming
Arrest us in mood enchanting,
Aqua transparent screens the dance
Of fish, leaving us in wordless trance.
The petal-like fish, soft and mellow
Form traffic in tubs to and fro.

Fling A Coin....

Loathsome, filthy and languid am I
Alongside the footpath so helplessly
Crying, look here, fling a coin, kiddo!

Like a leaf dry in cyclone, blown forlorn
I suffer and suffer until dusk from morn
Look here kiddo the world doth me scorn!
Day in and day out I suffer and die
A living death seeking Time's mercy
For redemption through Death
from aching penury!
This wayside the people without a sigh
Glimpse me, hearts unmoved pass by,
I beg you kiddo, put a coin kindly!
Kindly my darling playful, blithe and gay
Bent I am with age filled with dismay
Don't you fling a coin, hope you may!

Florid Poem

Shall I write now and sing!
A poem like mind's quivering
Shall I create a florid poem?
As a bird flits across the sky bloom
And a fish moving in aquarium
In the blues cape rain splashes
There the lightning lashes
Shall I poetize pleasure and pain?
With the same state and strain
Poem is but a sigh and question
Defying any answer to mention.

Fondling Breeze And

Forest Beckoning

Waving fields green in a sunny day
Beckons, feast your eyes it may.
Azure mountains in snow-capped majesty
Attract your mind behind veil misty.
Yonder the forest with its mantle deep
Calls upon your soul in peace to keep
Look at the arch of rainbow across the sky.
Though colorful, it looks motionless lying lazy.
Softly the breeze fondles the thick forest
Where the animal kingdom takes warm rest
The birds forget to chirp, sleep along
Until the warm rays awaken
the notes of the song.

Fragrance After Drizzle

The strings of pearl cut by breeze
Fall as rain-drops in all ease;
The moistened earth blushes green
With richness celebrating the scene;
Blooming and poignant her countenance
Smears wondrous thrill, the fragrance;
The muddy earth spreads incense;
Maddening, alluring the smelling sense;
Drenched earth by the sweet showers
Is worth a thousand flowers:

From Gloom To Bloom

There the seller of dolls and toys
Calls upon the kids, girls and boys
The young swarmed at him gladly

But the seller felt so badly
For he was blind, not to see
The colorful toys he sold to kids' glee!
The young and their parents paid him right
Exact price for toys looking bright
Around him in the daylight bustle
Ambiance so filled with wonder and puzzle
The seller felt a joy ineffable
Consoled himself, and so able
To steer clear the unfortunate gloom
And go along the tide of joy and bloom.

From Sordid To Sublime

I shall put all in a string
Of verbal melody and sing!
All the stray pearls and gems
Of experience created from sordid whims.
I sublimate them into a luminous plane.
Every grain would not go in vain,
As the alchemy transforms the base
Metal into costly luster to gaze
Bubble like things grow into pebble
And then as diamond dazzling marvel!
The poet's pen scribbles into to splendid
A thing that is otherwise banal, candid!

From The Stony Silence

The sculptor's chisel wakes up
Hitherto unknown image
From the stony silence

There arises a creation
Of a frozen state fluid memories
The image born of chisels pat deft stroke
Stands, casts a spell
On the passer by!
Who heaves a sigh?
Someone greeted the sculptor
The image emerging seemed to articulate
Am I not to be prayed?
Meanwhile chisel's note of melody
Pervaded in the air,
Cling the chisel doth sing!

Hail Dreams

Dreams deck and honor
Hail dreams!
Lovers' domain of
Life with openness and
Shy eloquence,
When the world of reality
Throws bitter threat
Dreams have rescue and reward.
After the candle is burnt fully,
The light enters in timid gestures.
And then the lovers greet,
Each other revels, in bliss.
No trace of shadows of
Frightful pain
As it is the unique domain
Hail the dreams
Every time they adorn and
Console one's life-breath.

How Dharma Charka Became Dharma Chakra

The dignity of India is hit.
India is sobbing helplessly,
As the ruthless hands of
Dussasan, the villain called
ADHARMA
Disrobed her!
Let us not wait for the
Advent of Lord Krishna, the
Lord of Souls.
Let us weave and deck
India with the apparel of
Dharma in our daily life and
Committed duty for her!
Gandhiji emerged in modern world
He is Krishna, serving and guiding
After shedding untruth
Throwing away the flute of Maya-illusion,
The warp and woof is
Truth and non-violence that
Flow to protect the garment of India.
We owe to Gandhiji the great redeemer
That held the chakra of Dharma
Spinning yarns from the
Cotton of native spirituality!
Thus Charkha became
The Chakra of Dharma!

How I Wish

I saw a rose radiant in the morn
How I wish it has no hurting thorn!
I stood on the shore of the tumultuous sea
I wish seagull's would fly along in glee.
As I see the cluster of stars in sky
I wish I could count them whimsically.
I wish to see two crescents in a while
As I behold twin tusks of the elephant, smile
Wishes a few come true at times,
The Bell of luck rarely chimes!

Hues

Still the mind
Instill the mind big
In still mind
You will find
Silence is eloquent.
Experience rich
Inward bliss
Beyond all exuberance
All commotion
All emotion
Die into space inner
Be one with ether,
Breathe in rhythm
Welcome the thought of non-entity.
Dissolve ego and
Solve the knot of illusion.
Come out of
The usual living

See yourself
Out of mind prism-
All hues disciplined
On the spectrum still!

Inner Vision

Oh! Men, who remain
Prisoners under the canopy
Blue and vast!
You are wriggling without
Wings of wisdom!
You are bereft of inner vision
As the elemental dance of the creator,
Presents all a riddle unraveled.
Are you in tune with your own?
Being?
Or straying away from it
You have not quenched your
Endless thirst.
Maybe you are all caught
In a Labyrinth!
Whom do you search for?
Ultimately!
Would you reach the destination?
Or end in thin air?
Time is but a poem unread.
Life is the rhythm ringing!
Do you read the poem?
And listen to the poetic rhythm!

It Seems

It seems
I should be
Soft as petal
Strong as metal
To write on
Man, God and life!
It seems
I should be
Humble as a child
To wonder
The Moon,
And the star-sown sky.
It seems
I should be
A busy bee
In love's bower
To sing, or never!
Ridges and bridges
Call upon
To sing on and on!
It seems
I should belong
To every planet
To cast the verbal net!

Journey

'i' is the horizon,
'I' is the sky!
From micro to macro
Soul travels from ego
to nameless vista!

The journey is endless
One can add and plus!

Kite
Flown is the kite in air
Looks in azure sky, fair
It has more than one tail
In the blue space doth sail!
The boy holds the thread tight
Adding color to the sky bright
Until it gets trapped in tree
Kite does not sink, it's free.
Look yonder the cloud dark
Kite penetrating doth embark
For a moment see its hides
Kite designed then soars and glides.

Laser Of Wisdom
Vision is blurred by layer thin
That is called cataract that sets in.
- It is like the misty film-
Laser of wisdom removes the cataract
And enables glimpse truth intact.
The inward eye needs to be
Free from the blur finally!

Lashing Rain
Water-proof shoes I wore

Along stream's shore
The rain I didn't foresee
My Mom warned repeatedly.
As I came out rain lashed
On me it ruthlessly splashed
Rain poured from above
Drenching my cap and shoe
Wearing the cap in hue blue
Earth Mom presented gay view;
Looking at myself in fret
Mom said, "An umbrella
you did forget! "

Lit The Lamp

In the heart-cave illusory
Darkness resides.
The cave is grim in grave silence.
Lit the lamp of Meditation.
It would issue glow and flow.
The light without wick and oil
Would not falter and flicker!
Hail the light of the domain inner.

Little One In The Cradle

Your charm bewitches words beyond
Like the lotus bud in the crystal pond!
As I push the cradle forward and back
You laugh like the duck's quack!
Your beauty graces the cozy cradle
We meditate on a lullaby and fondle!
O! Little one dear charming child

Our minds mad with joy go wild!
Memory of the mundane living fleets
As the little one's smile unique greets!

Log On With 'You'

Within you
There is the sky
Ever widening.
Look into you.
From that space
Look at you-the outer sheath.
The real you
The inner view.
The big you
Is all view
Transcend the
Mask, the small you.
The living petty
You must reach
Beyond it
Living, into
Nothingness?
Go beyond
For fullness
Conquer the Matter
Grasp the Force
The loss apparent
Is the Gain transparent!
Matter matters not
While the soul
Is the matter sole!

Love's Splendor

Love's splendor friendly gesture
Provide the naked soul vesture
Passion and being are full of charm
Petty things do not harm!
Dream of thorny woods now fled
Beyond hatred, beckons love's floral bed
Love the child help the soul - mate
Nature maternal comes to sublimate
Then all life is sacrament, game
Well-played beyond reproach and fame
Loneliness hatred are erased no trace
Of such darkness on Bliss's Face!

Loving Gestures

The teacher wished to
And children went to the zoo.
Fun and fear were in fusion
For a moment joyous confusion.
Kids found frightened at lion's roar
Birds beckoned them with colours galore!
One of the kids wondered to see
The peacock's feather joyfully.
Dappled and designed
with thousand eyes
The bird was a feast fond and nice.
One wondered what if one can
Pluck a feather from the gorgeous train!
"Don't pluck the feather from the train
It would harm the bird in pain.
The peacock gorgeous with loving gesture

Might shed feathers full of lustre",
So a little kid willingly said
"Wait for the peacock to shed".

Mind-Canvas

Tides mount in speed on sea
Tending to touch farthest sky,
But to oblige shore's silent plea!

Garlands of words do make
Poetry, filling aroma in readers' mind
All words for harmony's sake

Emotion-dipped brush so soft
Runs to depict imagination's riot
Only to keep mind-canvas aloft.

My Sweet Afar

Diving for pearls
In mendicant's tears
I weave a wreath of stars
I come to you, my sweet afar.
Gathering wine
From women's lips
And honeyed children's looks
I come to you, my sweet afar.
In dark of dusk
I scrape all hues
Of day's rich husk
I come to deck, my sweet afar.
I wring sweet tunes

From leaping streams
For you to dance in trance
As you are my giddy sweet afar.
I churn fairy lights
From little children's
Rhapsodical eyes
For you have to blaze,
my sweet afar.

Myself A Sea-Gull

I threw the net in the ocean of experience,
on the bank of life.
The net is but my poetry;
I sat on the chill soft sand.
Contemplating, I sat on the shore of life.
I cast the net, yonder i see the waves
of the sea appearing like the waving green fields.
And the foam and surf of the sea
Resembling the grains at the top,
in the fields of the ocean's coast.
The sea-field has the eternal harvest
ready with the surf grains.
To be reaped by the sea-gulls
flying like the silver-sickles
I will also love the sea of life
let me become a sea-gull
Wading and flying through- singing
the song of the surging sea of life;

Name It

Breeze wooed and whispered
In the rustle

Of the ear-leaves
Of the tree:
"I love dear"
The tree in a mood,
Self forgetful,
Spoke to the breeze;
"I pine for you"
So, the breeze replied
"You are the tree pine".

Nature Mom's Law

In all majesty elephant treads
The track as the green mantle spreads
Forest wears new fine look
Amidst deep wood runs the brook
Birds chirp their notes at will
And the song warble is presented through bill.
Elephant in its trunk, curly arm
Smells the moistened earth and feels warm
Looks at the tender bamboo shoots
Steps near thicket and loots
Elephant doth enjoy eating the bamboo tender
Who will stop the mighty greedy figure?
Alas! What it would be?
Bamboo would perish
Nature's law makes the bamboo
grow again to flourish!
For in a day or two insipid
the shoots would be
From the elephants bite
the bamboo is spared free
The tasteless bamboo thrives,
shoots skyward

Mother Nature's law saves
as a rescuing guard!

Nature's Charm Fascinating
Distant hills look like soft tides
Sylvan beauty mist draped, forest hides
Its trees creepers in emerald green
The roar of falls breaks silence unseen
Then the lashing lightning across cloud
Hits in a flash, against the dark shroud
Though momentary charms of nature unfold
Only to free our mind,
rescue from the ennui held!

New Year Plan
It shall be happiness joy and fun
When you will shoot with camera and not gun
Radiate love and it's warm light
Forget petty things and frightful fight
Varied skin! Look from within.
Humanity is one family kith and kin?
Colors different coexist on dolphin
Color and hue commune in soul and skin.
Under the sky-roof we make a clan
In this NEW YEAR this is our choice plan.

Not Wet....
I learn from everything
Yes,

From even banal thing
The shore lifted me apparently.
Alongside, the stream
Flows with ripples
Circles, largely written
On sheet (of water)
As it flows gently, softly
My shadow falls on!
My shadow falling on the stream
Not drenched or wet.
Let my mind stay
Sun-drenched with desire and dismay!

Notes And Hues

Notes and Hues
Cuckoo sang to the notes of flute
Awakening my heart-strings hither to mute
The flash of lightning in blue heavens!
Lifts me from slumber sordid, a song to commence
I glimpse yonder hues of the rainbow
It gives florid color poesy's glow.
Tides of boisterous breakers sing.
To say, life is leaping up, for shore less
rejoicing!

One And All

The thin ripple along seashore
Whispered softly, " I love you more "
Wavering breeze whispered into petal-ear,
I wandered in search of you my dear,
The creeper anxious with silent love,

Embraces, the trunk in a pond furrow,
There the waterfalls boisterous call
Abundant love announcing for one and all.

Only To Give Back

Oyster's mouth opened in fond hope
Then rain made its way into sea as drop
The dreamy time passed slowly
Someone dived deep for the reward pearly!
The radiant sun-orb in broad sky
Bestowed the flower, gift of brilliance gladly
Then the flower gratefully returns in bower
Transforming the warm rays into myriad color
The prism of imagination, the poet's mind
Is rare gift of life, queer kind?
When life's light enters in poet's ken
He gives back in array spectrum's pattern!

Panda Bear

Panda bear sprightly panda bear
In chill weather left to bear.
The fur-coat panda doth wear
As gift from nature's loving care
Eats tender bamboo sprout
Panda tastes mushroom munching soft
The green shade and deep forest
Offer pandas a cool comforting rest.
Hither and thither panda glibly runs.
Clothed in fur without buttons
Happily hopping moving in the wood
Panda shares with cub its favorite food.

Paper Crowns

They hop and sing happily
Greet each other in glee!
Birthday the kids celebrate
Finding warm willing soul-mate
Paper crown they prefer to wear
Kids boisterous join fun and fare!
No trace of pain or frown.
They are one in paper crown
Kids establish the kingdom of God
The winds thrilled, bless with a nod!
Kids jump with joy and fun
Besetting boundaries they shun.
Together the kids warmly rejoice
Greet happy birthday in uniting voice!

Parrot In Cage

Krishna is dark
But is sun to my soul
My life's sole goal
Sea - wave's blaze
Krishna in every sweep
Entrancing rainbow's leap.
Krishna is first
In all creation's thirst
For all galaxies burst
Krishna is song serene
Enchanting worlds like witch
And stellar tunes enrich,
Dark, dark, eternally black

Krishna glooms in me
A bird caught in glee!

Penance

The sun beam flows mellow
As tides of saffron yellow
Bathing the lotus in pond;
Still stands enchanting
The lotus, her petals painting,
Looks like a dream.
Words beyond
Like a poet obsessed
Like a love confessed
Is the Lotus in trance?
Has she homage to offer
Secrets cherished to murmur
Standing in one-legged
Penance!

Proud Ogling Peacock

As you dance it doth fascinate
The soul of the frenzied female mate
In the train of feathers eyes galore
Unfolding color and hue splendor!
You dance in ecstasy spontaneously
At your will under cloudy canopy
You strut about unfurl Beauty!
Shed one or two feathers in glee
Bewitching eyes beckon us to see
Arrays of colors at once open
Blue green bluish tint and so on!

Feasting the painters' quizzical eye!
Befitting the crest on your head
Proud ogling attracts, ennui fled!

Rainbow

Rainbow
Is it the banner or festoon
hung in the heavens,
glorifying the rain?
When the sun-light and
the rain-filled clouds embrace -
Perhaps the fond impress
has brought the color-pattern!
Sit a silent communication saying
that the wealth withers in
The momentary mundane living;
Is it a painting on the canvas of sky?
Or is it a bow without a string!
Is it the dream of a virgin?
There are in the world, arrows galore
that would hurt and kill
But i behold the bow, amidst the clouds,
Dripping and dropping the life-giving arrows;
Hail the bow of peace in the world of turmoil
writhing desperate and restless;

Riddles

Is it the snake sneaking?
In the grove sylvan
It is but the river
Welcome by the trees

Greeting with dropping flowers
Night tries hatching
The moon-egg
In the attempt abortive
Sheds the dew-tears
Poor night-hen!
As the dark florist sea
Trying to sell surf-flowers,
None to smell and buy!
The writhing sea wails
Alas!

Ringed Parrot

Ringed parrot, ringed parrot!
Picking, eating sweet carrots!
Chirps to greet when strangers meet!
Stays in wooden cage prattles,
reads a page?
As if in a book of rhymes
and trembles when bell chimes!
When i say, smile a while to click for photo-file,
Timid the parrot so it looks
says something, beyond books!
I offer to drink and eat
Fail not to fondle, greet!
The parrot shivers in fear
As the cat moves near!

Sect And Insect

Where knowledge is free

Horizons extend!
Brother and sister
In that ever-extending space
Flock together!
Though multi-hued are
Our feather!
Seeking and searching
Not exclusive and
Sectarian realms
Towards one world
With an air for breathing
Impulse and pulse should
Throb with fraternal bond!
Let us flock with wings of
Love and Liberty,
No sects and evils-dividing
Bards become Birds!
Where knowledge is free:
Even the harmonium that we play
Has a note of harmony,
Having reeds vibrant
And it reads the note of living.
The entire world is a fit abode
Where knowledge is free ….
No petty parochial division,
No duality, only fraternity.
My soul-mates!
You believe in peace and love!
If you believe in Sect
You are Insect!

Self And Self

From 'i' to 'I'
An eternal journey!
Drop to an ocean
Leaf to tree
Atom to universe
It is a religious verse!

Shall I Greet
I would like to
Award a prize
to the sleepless poet-sea
Singing all the time.
Shall give compliment
To one who decked the peacock
With plumage of hues galore.
I shall award a prize
To the Artist
Who introduced light and shade
And greet the gardener of the sky
I shall seek
For the Boy
Who kicked the sun-ball
To the west and award.
I shall congratulate
The Great Weaver
For Rainbow- banner.
I shall glorify
The great Soul
Who gave me the mind
And the soul to glimpse
And pay tribute to
All creations.

Soul Symphony.

The cat in man doth whine
Always me: Me: and Mine!
Clung in possession, Man though wise
Happy state changes otherwise
The cat ego braggart doth wish
Makes exit, peace to vanish.
But the cat's deceptive illusion
Is bereft of sharp glittering vision
The cat of ego casts a shadow
Those lies in being subtle, lo!
Can one burn or wash the shadow?
Rescue redemption from cosmic ego
Arrived in the inner being and so
The shadow cat whines no more
Only soul symphony, no furore!

Swing-Song

I go to and fro
Seeing high and low
Swing takes above
And safely below!
High and low on par
We feel not even in the car.
Swing and sing along
As fancies galore throng!
Hills and dales fascinate
Me! Nature turns my soul-mate
Inner being lost in thrill
Of movement and sweet will!

Teresa, The Saintly Mother

Orphaned, forsaken and disown destitute
Waited moaning, groaning and mute
Until the Touch Divine came to lift
From the listless lot, love bereft!
The dirty dismal hollow dust bin
For a moment sheltered
without kith and kin.
Worldly mother had thrown
disowning the child,
As the spiritual mother offered
care mellow mild!
Canonized soul has power and will
Help and listen to prayers still.
Did not the mother saintly say?
"Find this joy of sharing,
you too may! "

The Cosmic Self

i am I write, for I am
i feel humble, simply!
I shed off the capital state
If myself would be
One with vastness,
The soul-flower shall
Open to merge
Into fullness, I would
Project myself into the profile I,
The cosmic I!

The Fabulous Mine

Clouds gather deep and dark
Are adorned by VIBGYOR - arch!
Likewise though for a moment fleeting
Life must get art's noble greeting!
Color and charm of Fancy's domain
Bewitch, grip the ken so fine!
Material world cries mine, mine!
Men Forget ART the fabulous mine.
That wealth of art, if bereft
The whole earth poorer will be left!

The Jubilant Tide And
The Joyous Kids

Teacher surrounded by kids,
Tiny souls
Stood by the sea side!
There the play of tide
Bewitched and beckoned.
A child said, "May we fasten
Bubble and surf into a string of pearls?
"
The teacher quibbled, "No it will be
Impossible! "
"Let us go home,
it is twilight," said the teacher.
Kids jubilantly said "
we shall count the tides
One by one and see the last one
of the sea! "

Teacher stood, wonder struck.
Another juvenile voice proclaimed,
The sea lives up to reach the rim of the sky!
But another child wondered,
the sky remains calm
And voiceless!
The teacher too remained wordless along with
The kids boisterous and Nature, silent witness.

The Lily Pond

The sheet of water, the transparent pond
Looks beautiful, fine, woods beyond!
The pinkish lily smiles shed gladly
Its image on the sheet mirroring the lily!
The blue sky looks into the pond-mirror
The onlooker is treated with visual flavor.
The lily with soft tips of flower
Smiles in wide-open petal lips, wild wonder
Then shower sudden falls
Aquatic pitter patter
The sheet now is wrinkled water
The image of lily is but strange
An onlooker wonders at the aquatic change!

The Prattled Panchavarna Parrot

The parrot prattled
The mass and the elite
Gathered around.
The parrot uttered:
My message is as old as the hills
But one and all found it,

Uphill task while trying to
Emulate Truth
They listened and listened
The parrot treated all alike,
Said, all are leaves of the same tree
The parrot was true to its prattle:
My life is my message
Simple for ears
Beyond grasp and grip
In real living
One day cat emerged
And sneaked
Frenzied and fanatic
Crafty and cunning
The cat snatched the parrot
Alas! a victim that wore
The look assumed the five varnas
(colours of fivefold caste)
The panchavarna parrot of
The Sanadana clan.
The parrot that try to unite,
Ignite the fire of brotherly love
Finally fallen a prey helpless
On the land tarnished with
Violence and duality.

The Swinging Soul

The question put to me
By myself is this:
Who writes poetry?
Is it the silence in you?
Or the pattern found

in the melody of words?
In their arrangement!
Whether Experience
Seeks for a
Voice of Being
That is married to musical words!
Or something complete in the listener's mind
That finally matters!
Questions swarm at
As scathing as waves in
boisterous.
In the inmost being
The poetic soul swings between
Silence and melody!

There Falls The Shadow

The sun peeps
Out in the sky
Creates shadows
Big and small!
What is the
Stuff or thing
Called shadows?
In the morn things
Called shadows
Assume shapes
At sun's will
They crawl grow
Then shrink
The shadows
Fall on waters,
Not drenched!

But all in black
They appear.
The sunlight
Seems to fling and
Throw.
The sun calls back
At the fall of dreamy
Dark Dusk, which, just
Swallows the shadow
In grim silence.
The sun wakes the
Shadows galore
When the flowers laugh
And smile at
The fall and rise of
The shadows!

Time Is A Wonderful Maid

Time is a wonderful maid!
She is changing her name daily
As- "Yesterday" "Today" and "Tomorrow"!
She never stops her travel
Like wind and river, moving always,
Her journey is on, on and on!
Time is a wonderful maid!
A virgin maid forever and ever;
Then and now I have seen her beauty
Here and there I have observed it;
Desire is my brush to hold it with grip
Here and there, in my heart
Which is a screen, to preserve it?
I am drawing with my might.

In her beautiful forehead
She keeps dark night as a dot;
The marble moon is
Her adorable face;
Perpetually she preserves her youth
Everlastingly young,
She never becomes old;
The morning star is a flower for her
She decorates her head with it
Before the dawn blossoms;
The bright color of the morning
Becomes the turmeric paste for her
After applying it for face
She plucks the evening sun
And puts it in her forehead
As a beautiful Tilak.
She covers her face
With fog as a veil;
After a while
She rises again
Like an awesome painting!
Oh! Eternal beauty!
The red sky in the dusk
She takes with much pleasure
To adorn her feet as a red paint!
The early night darkness
Is a cosmetic ointment
For her eyes;
Time - a wonderful maid
Never becomes old
Like a poem highly classic
She lives a life of eternity!
The rhythmic musical sound of rivers
Is it a wonderful tribute for her?

The spring, full of flowers, is the
Enchanting smile of the maid, Time!
The Fame which never withers,
Remains as her friend forever!

Toys

Toys beautiful we do sell
With them children play very well
Funny big toys talk and sing
Birds' colorful striking wing!
Horns and caution bells sound
Onlookers attracted attention bound!
Elephant, Giraffe stout Pig
As in zoo small and big
Bears dark with bushy fur
Leopard, Lion, Deer, Tiger.
The Parrot's bill bent so nice
Toys tagged to slips of price
.Come and buy girls and boys
You may safely keep the toys!

Transforming The Ignoble…

Lord Buddha wandered searching Truth
Renouncing royal living, gone forth!
And the Master went from door to door
With a begging bowl, pomp no more!
Stood like a painting calm and stately.
Lord tranquil, observed silence quietly!
From inside the house a lady vociferous
Uttering ignoble words
to ears pious brought food.

Tarry a little, the Lord merciful softly said
If I refrain from accepting the offering, O Maid!
Who would own it, kindly say?
With a nod she uttered,
"Certainly I may! "
Thus if I don't accept words unrefined
Who shall own? Hearing words kind
The land-lady got enlightened!
Prostrated solemnly at the feet noble
Repenting for her blunder is terrible!

Under The Greenwood..

The woods are green for bird and beast
Offering shade safe and feast
If man goes with axe to fell
Arid dry will become earth dismal
Sky-canopy moans in silence
As the earth erased of greenery
By wordless violence the axe's folly
Flower fruit and the song of the birdie
All a banquet provided by trees naturally
Sit, smile at Nature's maternal lap
Then look for a laptop and world-map!
Before the green images go fleeting
Capture, house them in laptop greeting!

Virtue, The Armor

Life is indeed a battlefield
To compulsion and compromise I yield!
Glibly what I imagined to be,
The game was otherwise surprising to me!

Preparing guarding myself for war
Moved forward to make or mar.
The sword of intellect, I wield so strong
Against many dark ills that throng!
In spite of sword's mightier rig
I found life's challenge big!
Besides swords glitter and sway
To guard myself from attack and slay
I thought I would wear the armor
Of VIRTUE to protect in all fervor!

Voice Of Oneness

Leaf, bud or charming flower
Enjoy breathing air of oneness in bower
Together: not to divide or dissect
Oneness should pave to eschew narrow sect
Dolphin suggests in a silent gesture
By wearing black and white skin-vesture!
No more differences apparent transient
Should mar love's law ancient
Under the blue calm rim of sky
Boisterously singing, leaps up the mating sea!
The creepers encircle the trunk of tree
Thus sharing fond embrace free!
Unfettered by dead convention live afresh
Life's lesson, learn in the mortal mesh.
Look from within, Mind-cup's open mouth
Then there shall be no north or south!

Voice Of Poesy

Silence interlacing tunes
It is a feast to loot:
Darkness in eye
Turn the pupil's light.
Mist roams to net a star
But defeated it sinks to earth:
Human difference a misty net
Amaze our brows.
The image in heart sailed the sea
Of poetry's realm all glee:
Heights and depths a mirage-
Amuse our fancy.
Scholar's heart is shore
Creator's mind a store
And poetry plying river's floods
A lightning weaves in starry buds.

Wealth Of Art

Clouds gather deep and dark
Are adorned by VIBGYOR arch!
Likewise, though for a moment fleeting
Life must get art's noble greeting!
Color and charm of FANCY'S domain
Bewitch, grip the ken so fine!
Material world may cry mine, mine!
Forgetting Art fabulous as mine
That wealth of Art if, bereft
The whole earth poorer will be left!

Wipers Of Equanimity

Pearly rain drops fall on glass

Blur the driver's vision across
The car of life we drive on and on
Until the destination farthest forlorn
When the roads picture is misty and dim
Moment leaves us serious and grim
Rain drops signify tears of joy and pain,
Both roll down the cheeks and mien
Wipers oscillate constantly to brush.
The drops, tears of pain fulfilled wish
As we regain the poignant vision clear.
We perceive, steer CAR far and near.

Wringing Tunes

Diving for pearls
In mendicant's tears
I weave a wreath of stars
I come to you, my sweet afar.
Gathering wine
From women's lips
And honeyed children's looks
I come to you, my sweet afar.
In dark of dusk
I scrape all hues
Of day's rich husk
I come to deck, my sweet afar.
I wring sweet tunes
From leaping streams
For you to dance in trance
As you are my giddy sweet afar.
I churn fairy lights
From little children's
Rhapsodical eyes

For you have to blaze, my sweet afar.

/The End/